VOTE!

A GUIDE FOR YOUNG ADULTS

★ AMY ESKIND ★

Why you should participate in our democracy and how to do it.

★

ABOUT THE AUTHOR

AMY ESKIND covers politics and political issues as a freelance journalist. Her work has appeared in *People* magazine, NPR, *Washington Post, Los Angeles Times, Nashville Scene, Tennessean*, and other publications. In 2017, she drove across the country to discover why 40 percent of the electorate didn't vote in the 2016 presidential election. What she learned informed this book. Eskind lives in Park City, Utah.

CONTENTS

Millions of young adults don't vote.

In the 2020 election, only half of eligible voters age 18 to 29 cast a legal ballot, and that was a stunning turnout. In 2022, a midterm year without a presidential election, youth turnout fell to 23 percent, and in five states less than 15 percent voted.

This book is intended to convince you to raise that statistic and vote. In every election.

If you are between the ages of 18 to 21, you have the opportunity to vote because some courageous people fought for your right to do it. During World War II, the United States lowered the draft age to 18, but those same teenagers being sent off to war had no right to vote for the leaders making military decisions. Some advocates fought for a lower voting age, but it didn't happen until decades later.

During the Vietnam War, 2.2 million men were drafted, 58,200 lost their lives, more than 150,000 were maimed, and another 1,600 went missing. It was an unpopular war, but young men in the U.S. could be forced into battle. Again, it seemed unfair. If their country's leaders could send them off to war, young people should be allowed to choose those leaders. A law was passed in 1970, an amendment to the Voting Rights Act of 1965, lowering the voting age to 18, but four states sued to block it and the Supreme Court found that the new federal law could only apply to federal elections. A Constitutional amendment would have to pass in order for 18-year-olds to have the right to vote in state and local elections, and getting a Constitutional amendment passed is notoriously hard to accomplish. Yet the 26th Amendment, lowering the voting age to 18, passed both houses of Congress, and was ratified by the states in just four months — a record — becoming law in 1971.

If you are 18, 19, or 20 today, you have the right to vote because many people put pressure on the federal government to change the law.

Don't take it for granted. A 2024 Republican candidate for President, Vivek Ramaswamy, has proposed passing a new Constitutional amendment raising the voting age to 25 unless a person passes a civics test or enlists for six months of public service. He calls it "civic duty voting." Not that this is likely to pass, but it could.

Advocates worked for decades to give women the right to vote, and to give Blacks the right to vote. In fact, the Founding Fathers only gave the right to vote to white men, and in some states they had to be land owners too. But relentless activists thought it was important that you have the right to vote in free and fair elections. They gave you power many people in other countries in the world do not have. They gave you, an ordinary citizen, the right to have a say in what happens in your city or town, state, and country.

If you are age 18-29, you are bound to care a lot about at least one political issue. What do you wish would be changed? Is your employer offering 12 weeks of paid paternal leave with job protection? No? A new law could require employers to offer that. Is the homeless population in your city worrisome? Your city and state governments could choose to spend more to address the problem. Are public school teachers underpaid in your town? Is the skyrocketing cost of prescription drugs crushing your budget? What about student loans? Are you worried about police brutality, but your city government just abolished citizen review boards? Do you wish there were more gun restrictions? Easier access to birth control, abortion pills or clinical abortions? Less access? More electric vehicle charging stations? More renewable energy? You get the idea. It's all politics. Vote for people who promise to work on issues that matter to you and who seem to have workable solutions you favor.

There are many reasons why youth don't vote. Here are some common ones:

"I go to school in a different state from where I live."
The state in which you go to school is where you actually live. Register to vote there. If you don't have a driver's license in that state, there are other forms of ID you can use. Go to vote.gov or vote.org to look up the registration rules and deadlines in your state. Alternatively, you may be able to vote absentee by mail in your home state. Just remember, you can't vote in two states.

"I just moved here and I'm not really aware of local political issues or candidates."
When you move, you become a resident of a new city or state. Educate yourself on local issues as fast as you can because local laws and local politics will affect you immediately. Are property taxes increasing? Is abortion severely restricted? Is city government investing in bicycle infrastructure? Is it business-friendly there or are companies leaving the area? Is the police department doing a good job keeping the public safe? Are the schools, colleges, and universities adequately funded? Does the court system seem fair? Is the city managing climate risks, such as flooding, wildfires, drought, and heat waves?

Even if you don't immerse yourself in local issues, still register to vote. Find out immediately how to register to vote. Many states allow you to register when you get a driver's license or even a library card.

Your participation in state and federal elections could affect the balance of power in your state legislature and the U.S. Congress. The majority party leads all of the committees for that body and decides which bills to discuss and bring to a vote. By casting a ballot for your elected officials, you could help sway an election, and that could change who is in the majority and what your state and the country's priorities are. It goes without saying that your vote matters in presidential elections too, as the winner also determines the country's priorities for the next four years.

"I don't feel informed enough, and I don't want to be wrong."
You absolutely should be informed before you vote. Go beyond ad campaigns. Do some research and try to figure out which candidates best match your priorities. There is no wrong answer, and it's no one's business how you voted – unless you decide to talk about it.

"No one asked me for my vote."
Campaigns typically do a lousy job of reaching young voters because they have a limited amount of funds and the best bang for their buck is going to be targeting likely voters. As a young person, and a person who has little to no track record of voting, you're not considered a "likely voter." That's okay, you can build up that track record by voting. For now, you'll have to seek out information and educate yourself about candidates and issues.

"I live in Alabama, Mississippi or New Hampshire. We don't have early voting and I can't get off work on election day."
Find out if you can apply for absentee voting at vote.org.

"I don't have transportation to my polling place."
Go to this helpful website: rideshare2vote.com.

Why does it matter so much whether young people vote?

When you don't vote, the people who get elected to make our laws may not address the issues that are important to you. Let's take gun violence. If the majority of people in the U.S. are in favor of an assault weapons ban, why hasn't it happened already?

In many states, legislators and governors have refused to pass any gun laws that restrict the Second Amendment right to bear arms, even after mass shootings. Many citizens groups and political non-profit organizations are demanding it. But when a wide swath of citizens fail to vote for legislators and governors who agree with their stance, their voices aren't heard where it matters – at election time. In states such as Texas and Tennessee, millions of eligible voters don't vote and therefore don't vote out elected officials who won't fix the problem. And elected officials count on that. Their loyalists will vote and keep them in office. No need to bend to the will of the majority to keep their jobs.

Why doesn't Tennessee Governor Bill Lee and the state legislature represent their constituents on issues such as gun control and abortion access? Let's look closely at Lee's election. In 2018, Bill Lee won in a landslide victory, but less than half of the state's 5 million eligible voters cast a ballot. If those millions who didn't vote had actually picked a candidate that aligned with their values and priorities and cast a ballot, Bill Lee may or may not be governor. Almost half of registered voters in Tennessee disapprove of the state legislature, but most didn't vote for their state representatives.

The consequence: following a devastating school shooting and loud public outcry for more gun control, the Governor issued an executive order to enhance reporting used in background checks for firearms purchases. Yet a vast majority of Tennesseans are demanding the state pass a red-flag gun law as well. The legislature isn't budging. A majority of voters think abortion should be legal when the life and health of the mother is at stake. Yet again, the legislature and the Governor are ignoring what a majority of their constituents want and have not amended their total abortion ban.

If more people paid attention to candidates at election time and if more people voted, would we be governed by people who more closely represent our values? Likely so, but there's only one way to find out: increase the vote.

There was a poignant ad that ran during the 2018 mid-term election, "Dear Young People, Don't Vote." (youtube.comtiwatch?v=t0e9guhV350). A series of older folks promised they would vote, and stressed that they didn't care about climate change ("that's a you problem, I'll be dead soon"), nor diversity and inclusion ("I can't keep track of whose life matters"), nor gun violence ("Sure, school shootings are sad. But I haven't been in a school for 50 years"). They smirk and say they know the young people won't vote. It is a striking ad because it's true. Turnout among older voters is much higher than among young people, and their priorities are different. If you want your priorities addressed, you know what you have to do.

Why does it matter so much if I vote? I'm only one person.

Every vote matters. In 2000, the presidential election between Al Gore and George W. Bush was so close it wasn't called for weeks. The tally came down to one state — Florida — and Gore ultimately lost by 537 votes to Bush. It was so close that the race was called for one and then the other, led to recounts and lawsuits, and ultimately ended up at the U.S. Supreme Court, which denied an additional selective recount, effectively handing the election to Bush. The issue in Florida was that when people voted, the voting machines made holes in a paper ballot next to their choice, but not all of the holes went all the way through and it was hard to tell the true intention of the voter. What a mess! Yes, every vote mattered. One polling place in Florida with better voting machines could well have swayed the entire election Gore's way.

The 2000 election was also interesting because Gore won the sum total of all the votes in the country — the "popular vote" — but lost in the electoral college. More people voted for Gore, but once a winner is declared in a state it doesn't matter how many extra votes they receive. So Gore over-achieved in some states, receiving more votes than he needed to win those states. However, with the electoral college system, it only matters how many states he won, and how many electoral votes each of those states awarded to him.

This comes up again and again, with one candidate winning the popular vote and another candidate winning in the electoral college. In 2016, that's exactly what happened. Despite the fact that Hillary Clinton won the popular vote by more than 2.8 million votes, Donald Trump won the electoral college by winning three swing states — Pennsylvania, Wisconsin and Michigan — that could have gone either way. In Pennsylvania, Trump won by just 44,292 votes. That's right! In Wisconsin, he won by 22,748 votes. In Michigan, he won by only 10,704 votes. The margins of Trump's win were minuscule. Every vote mattered. And yet, 3.5 million eligible voters didn't cast a legal ballot in Pennsylvania, 1.3 million didn't cast a legal ballot in Wisconsin, and 2.6 million people didn't cast a legal ballot in Michigan in that election. If those 7.4 million people had voted, who knows how the entire election would have gone. The margins were so slim that out of 136,753,936 total votes in the election, Trump won by less than 78,000 votes in three states. Miniscule. It all came down to who cast a legal ballot.

Why does it say cast "a legal ballot?" Some votes are thrown out because signatures can't be verified, a voter forgot to bring a valid ID, the address on the registration is incorrect, or some other mix-up. These voters are given a provisional ballot, but if they neglect to return to clear up the problem, their votes are not counted. Some 750,000 provisional ballots were not counted in 2016.

In the 2020 presidential race, Joe Biden won Georgia by less than 12,000 votes. More than two million Georgians didn't cast a legal ballot. In Arizona, Biden won by 10,457 votes, while a million-and-a-half eligible voters didn't cast a legal ballot. Because so many states are divided so narrowly, margins can be tiny, and each person who doesn't correct their provisional ballot forfeits their chance to help sway an election.

You never know when your vote will make all the difference.

Here's another example. In 2022, Rep. Cindy Axne, an Iowa Democrat, lost her seat in the U.S. House of Representatives by just 2,145 votes. The winner in the race, Zach Nunn, a Republican, helped tilt the balance of power in the House to Republicans, who clinched the majority by less than a dozen seats out of a total of 435. Every one of the eligible voters in that Iowa congressional district — including those who voted and those who didn't — all contributed to the change in majority party of the entire House of Representatives.

When votes are finished being counted and winners are announced in each race, it is determined which party has the majority in the House and Senate. As stated earlier, the party that holds the majority of seats is given the right to appoint their members as chair of every House and Senate committee. So if Republicans win the House, as they did in 2022, every House committee is lead by an appointed Republican. Priorities are set by that leader — which issues are discussed, which bills come up for a vote, and which people or agencies will be investigated. In the Senate, the party in power leads confirmation hearings for agency heads and federal judges who have a big impact on our daily lives. The Secretary of Transportation, Administrator of the EPA, and Supreme Court Justices are some of the leaders nominated by the President who must then be confirmed by the Senate.

Today, a majority of Supreme Court justices are conservative and decisions by the court lean conservative. That's how Roe vs. Wade, the Supreme Court decision that gave women in every state the Constitutional right to an abortion, was tossed after almost 50 years. How did conservatives win the majority on the Court? By controlling the White House and the Senate when Supreme Court seats became vacant.

Republicans held the majority in the Senate when a seat became vacant during former President Obama's last year of office, and they exercised their power to refuse to hold a confirmation vote on Obama's Supreme Court nominee. They said voters in the upcoming election should be allowed to vote first, hoping they could win the presidency and fill the seat with a judge chosen by a Republican president who would undoubtedly lean conservative.

After Trump became President, he was given the opportunity to fill two Supreme Court seats, and then a third was rushed through Senate confirmation just before an election — the very thing the Republican Senate wouldn't let Obama do. But, again, they were in the majority, which gave them that power. That tilted the court to conservative. President Trump couldn't have done it without his party holding the majority of seats in the Senate.

Each eligible voter who cast a legal ballot for a Senate candidate, and each eligible voter who didn't, contributed to the new conservative lean of the Supreme Court. By having the power of the vote, ordinary citizens like you decide who sits in the U.S. Senate – and that can make a world of difference. It all starts with you. Your vote is powerful.

Seems like a lot of shouting. I'm not into politics.

You are already into politics, whether you know it or not. If you live in the United States, you depend on the federal government to set domestic policies and diplomacy with other countries, and defend our country militarily. You depend on the government to protect your civil rights. And to study and inform public health. To run airports and pass laws about air travel that are intended to keep you safe. You depend on state government to keep up the highways, state parks, public schools and universities, public safety, and environmental stewardship. Your state government also makes and enforces statewide civil and criminal laws. State governments run elections and make election rules, such as whether eligible adults can register to vote on election day, or if they must register as much as 30 days prior. And that's just a partial list.

A Houston man, who insisted he wasn't political, pulled ruined furniture out of his house after a massive flood. His house was built on a flood plain, a designated area where the government has determined that flooding is likely. Somehow, a developer got permission to build there, and this man moved in. He was waiting for the Federal Emergency Management Agency (FEMA) to inspect his property and hopefully give him money to cover the damage to his house. That is political! This whole story is political. A floodplain was designated by the government, the city issued building permits allowing this neighborhood to be built on the floodplain, and the homeowner expected the federal government to bail him out. It's all politics.

Which brings me to my next point. It absolutely makes a difference who is in charge and what their priorities are. Will they do something to protect your city from flooding? If your city has flooded in the past, you probably want to know. Do they care about working people living paycheck to paycheck? Do they think the United States military should intervene in other countries' problems, or are they reluctant to get involved? What kind of judges will they nominate — judges who may or may not rule with impartiality, judges who have strong records on civil rights or criminal reform, or judges with so little experience it's hard to know how they will preside? Do they believe public money should help fund private education? Are they supportive of LGBTQ+ rights? Candidates for public office should be willing to share their views. If you listen closely, you'll see that your city and state and country can go in vastly different directions depending on who is elected to lead, and it's likely going to affect your education, your property, your business, your health, and more.

It feels like no one really cares about me or gets anything done that I'd like to see. President Biden promised to erase some of my student debt, and then he didn't (at least so far). Most of the country wants stricter gun laws yet Congress can't get it done.

It's not easy to pass new federal regulations and laws. Sometimes elected officials want to do something, such as have your student debt erased, and a judge may find it unconstitutional. Sometimes industries (think firearms manufacturers, the pharmaceutical industry, banks) that benefit from keeping things as they are now will spend big dollars to fight any changes. Sometimes groups of people opposed to a change will fight it. Sometimes the final product will be a watered-down compromise, and other times it will be impossible to make headway on the issue at all. It's a consequence of letting everyone have a say, which is a great concept but also messy.

Keep in mind too that issues evolve as people get more information and become more comfortable with the change. Take gay marriage. Polls showed that the country was against the idea a few decades ago. The more gay advocates told personal stories about the unfairness of not being given the rights and benefits afforded to straight married couples, the more the needle moved. It was a rocky road — some states said it was legal, and then challenges to the law made it illegal again. In 1996, Congress passed the Defense of Marriage Act, making it legal for states to deny gay marriage. More personal stories were told. Eventually, the country changed its collective mind, and many states recognized gay marriage. A Supreme Court decision in 2015 finally made same sex marriage legal throughout the country. Gay advocates had spent decades protesting and demanding their rights, and today's married gay couples will surely tell you it was worth the fight.

Just as others fought for or against change concerning the legality of gay marriage, you can advocate for or against change on issues that matter to you. Go to candidate forums, write to your elected officials, gather some like-minded people and stand outside your state legislature or the US Capitol with signs, grab some media attention (without doing anything illegal) and let your opinion be heard. Write a letter to the editor of your local newspaper. Support candidates with your money and time who promise to work on your issue.

You won't always get your way, and sometimes change takes a long, long time — sometimes decades — but if you don't vote and don't get active, you've squandered your opportunity. You've left the job of shaping laws that affect you to others

who may not be aware of your viewpoint or may simply dis-
agree with it.

It's your money.

Here's a quick primer on taxes. If you make enough money,
you likely owe some of it to the state (unless you live in a state
without state income taxes) and to the federal government. You
made it, they take a portion. How that money is spent is up to
the officials you and other voters elect. Elected officials decide
whether the police department will get more funding, or if
some will go to mental health counselors instead. They decide
whether we send money to Ukraine, boost military salaries, or
cut funding for state universities. Don't you want a say in who
gets to decide how your money is spent? When a candidate
runs for public office, they should tell voters what they will pri-
oritize, and if they don't, press them on it. Use the information
to decide who you want to dole out your money.

P.S. Your tax dollars also pay salaries for elected officials
and their staff. They literally work for you. How great that
you get to choose who to hire for the job.

Okay, but I've heard the Democrats and Republicans are both corrupt and I don't know where to turn.

Corruption comes in many forms, and there will always be
elected officials who do things they shouldn't. Hopefully their
misdeeds come to light and they are appropriately punished.
However, there are some very real, systemwide, foul-smell-
ing but legal funding issues in politics today. There is a limit
to what you can donate to a candidate or Political Action
Committee (PAC), but in 2010 the Supreme Court's Citizens
United decision allowed corporations and outside groups to

contribute unlimited amounts of money. Now corporations and mega-wealthy donors can give, give anonymously (what's known as "dark money"), and give to their heart's content to super-PACs and issue-oriented political non-profits. They can and do, for example, anonymously fund ads and postcards and mailers stirring fear about candidates they oppose.

Always keep in mind that it's up to us to demand new laws and stricter oversight of campaign finance.

If you'd like to look into who is funding particular campaigns through political donations, go to Open Secrets, opensecrets.org, a site run by an independent non-profit. There is a great deal of information there, but you will not find all of the contributors behind each group that donates to political campaigns because many contributors to political non-profits remain anonymous.

Changing the Supreme Court ruling that allows these anonymous or "dark money" political non-profit donations would require a new law by Congress. Though some have tried to make that happen, no such law has passed as of this writing. Those who benefit from it — current elected office holders — have no reason to curtail the funding stream. Fighting shady money in politics will take all of us.

Another word on money in elections. Ask any U.S. Representative or Senator and they'll tell you they spend a large portion of their time in office simply raising money. Billions of dollars are spent on these races by individual campaigns, political parties, and outside groups. Campaign expenses include advertising, staff, and travel, and when one candidate, their political party, and outside groups are spending big, the pressure is on other candidates to match them, making the price of running a competitive campaign exorbitant. Many people feel there is too much money in politics, and worry that politicians need so much money to run their campaigns that they need to take donations from special interest groups intent on having candidates do their bidding once in office. In other words, the fear is that the large donors can "buy" elected officials.

Ever feel that an unpopular elected official is vulnerable and probably won't win — and then they do? Chances are good an outside group, whose donors may never have stepped foot in your state, spent big to sway voters, often by making them fear the opponent. Their aim is to influence federal law and they want this office holder to be on their side.

Here's one solution that has been gaining momentum: small donor public financing. Rather than spending so much time coddling mega-wealthy donors and special interest groups that can send large checks, small dollar public financing gives candidates a way to raise what they need from average working people. Modest contributions are typically matched and multiplied many times over with public funds. For example, New York City offers a multiplier of eight for mayoral candidates, so a supporter's $250 donation is matched with public funds and is then worth $2,250 to a participating campaign. Seattle, Washington, and Oakland, California, have adopted a voucher program. Residents over age 18 are given four $25 vouchers to give to political candidates running for municipal offices. These programs result in candidates engaging with more constituents — and more diverse constituents — who are now making financial contributions. It also gives working people who are not wealthy and well-connected a better shot at competing for elected office.

Public funding programs typically require candidates to meet modest fundraising requirements and agree to limit total campaign spending in order to participate. This makes the public financing option a hard choice, since opponents not taking public funding will not have those limits. Nevertheless, political candidates around the country are choosing to participate.

Several states, cities and municipalities offer public financing for political campaigns. If yours is not one of them and you see this as a smart solution to corruption from big money in politics, you might join or start a group that is advocating for it.

Wasn't the 2020 election rigged or stolen? Why should I vote if it's all rigged?

Given the chance to contest the 2020 election, then-President Donald Trump and his lawyers could not come up with actual evidence that anything nefarious happened in that election. Trump and his lawyers kept promising they had evidence, but they never produced it during dozens of legal challenges, which they lost. Several of former President Trump's lawyers have already plead guilty to related crimes, essentially admitting they lied about the election being rigged. In conclusion, and despite what the ex-President continues to say about the 2020 election, the matter should have been put to rest. The election was not stolen.

A word on the media.

If you think the country is polarized now, you're right. It is reflected, or perhaps spearheaded, by our media outlets. News sources no longer sound neutral, just giving the facts. Many are partisans, either liberal or conservative, and slant the news for a segment of the population that believes the way they do. Some of the outlets play fast and loose with the truth, as the Dominion Voting suit proved about Fox News. Even Fox's own anchors didn't believe what they were broadcasting — that the voting machines were rigged. It's a sorry state for journalism and the public doesn't trust the media. Beyond that, social media doesn't consistently have the same standards as the major news media outlets, but it looks and feels authentic. Disinformation spreads easily.

Be aware that artificial intelligence (AI) can offer information that looks like it would be true but is not true. Photographs and videos can be doctored. The best advice is to use your noggin and find sources you trust to tell you the truth. The rest is just noise, and it can be alluring as well as deafening. Be smart about your media consumption, and don't feel you have to live in a "news silo" where you only hear information from one point of view.

The media is also partly to blame for a general lack of interest in local politics. Local news media used to offer extensive daily coverage of local issues and local political leaders. Today, local news is in decline, and many news consumers are more focused on national politics than local issues because they get regular updates on their phones, and it can be very dramatic and compelling.

The result is that few people bother to vote for mayoral races today. Less than half of registered voters in Los Angeles voted in the mayor's race in 2022. It's the second largest city in the United States, and you can be elected mayor with half a million votes. You can be mayor of New York City with just over 750,000 votes, as Eric Adams did in 2021. In fact, there are some 5 million eligible voters in New York City, the largest city in the nation, and only 1.1 million people voted for their own mayor. Most didn't vote, even as New York City was in the midst of a pandemic and a crime spree.

If you think something needs to change in your city, tell mayoral candidates about your concern, hear what they have to say about it, and choose carefully. You have the power to vote in and vote out your elected officials.

What's the difference between the parties?

Every election is different. Party platforms change and candidates pull out issues that are important at the time. One election might center on health care access, one on immigrants and refugees streaming in at the border. Shifting winds make it hard to generalize, but here goes.

In general, Republicans lean conservative, believe in a small role for federal government intervention, letting commerce lead. They are concerned with our ballooning federal deficit, and favor low taxes along with cuts to federal spending on social programs such as free school lunch and Medicare. They place an emphasis on individual freedoms, including the right to own a firearm. Fundamentalist religions find a home here, and advocate for such policies as banning abortion, banning books they find inappropriate, and using public funds for religious schools. Republicans have been slower to accept that climate change is caused by humans, and that we can and should do something about it.

Democrats tend to lean liberal, believing that the federal government exists to provide services and support to those who need it. Democrats tend to believe in the pregnant individual's right to make health care decisions with their doctor — including abortion — with some limits. They tend to support gun control, LGBTQ+ rights, a fairer tax system that would erase loopholes for the mega-wealthy, and they advocate for a transition to clean energy.

I don't align with Republicans or Democrats. What about other parties?

There are several other political parties in the United States besides the Democrat and Republican parties. Libertarian, Green, and Constitution parties, and many other smaller parties, may field candidates in major elections but they tend to lose to well-funded candidates from the two major parties.

The Libertarian Party is the largest of these, with a platform that includes abolishing the IRS (our tax collection agency), and promotes small government that interferes less in the economy and in people's lives. The Party also stands up for civil rights and individual freedoms. They've entered candidates in presidential elections but only garnered a small percentage of votes. They've had more success in state legislatures.

There are some newer parties, formed by people who dislike the two major parties and are seeking something more centrist and practical. The Forward party, founded by failed 2020 presidential contender Andrew Yang, is seeking to become a national centrist party. No Labels is another. The United Utah Party is an example of a state-only centrist party. There are many small parties in addition to those mentioned. There are socialist and communist parties, and others with a more narrow focus, such as the New African Black Panther Party.

Aside from organized political parties, candidates have the option to call themselves Independent. It can be harder for Independents to raise enough money to compete with candidates from major parties, but there have been some notable successes. As of this writing, there are three sitting U.S. Senators who consider themselves Independent. Bernie Sanders from Vermont is one, though he caucuses (meets to discuss bills) with the Democrats and ran for president as a Democrat. Two states have organized Independent parties, Delaware and Oregon.

The most recent independent candidates for president who made any strides were John B. Anderson in 1980 and H. Ross Perot in 1992. Anderson was a third place finisher, earning only 6.6 percent of the vote and losing to Ronald Reagan. Twelve years later, Perot ran as an independent and also finished in third place with a respectable 18.9 percent of the vote, losing to Bill Clinton. Even though people often say they are fed up with both major political parties, it's hard to win a national race without the funding and organization of the Democrat and Republican parties.

It's a good idea to familiarize yourself with the parties and choose where you align, especially if you live in a state that forces you to declare your affiliation when you register to vote. Check your state laws, but in many cases you can only vote in a primary election for the party in which you are registered. When it comes time to cast your ballot in the general election, you can vote for any candidate on the ballot regardless of your stated party affiliation.

Keep in mind that in the states where you must declare your party affiliation when you register to vote, it's easy to change your affiliation.

*Note: Sometimes third party candidates are considered spoilers, especially in presidential elections. A third party candidate who is widely considered to have no chance at winning may siphon votes away from a Democratic or Republican candidate and change the outcome of the election. You have every right to vote for such a candidate, but you may hear people say the candidate was a spoiler or that you wasted your vote.

Here's an example: Jill Stein ran as a Green Party candidate in the 2016 presidential race. Her voters were likely liberal. In Michigan, where the margin between Trump and Clinton was 10,704 votes, Stein got 51,463 votes. She never had a shot at winning, but if she wasn't on the ballot Clinton may have gotten at least 10,705 more votes (granted, some of the voters may have decided not to cast a ballot at all) and that may have changed the outcome of the election, handing the state to Clinton. Stein voters in Pennsylvania and Wisconsin similarly could have closed the gap for Clinton. That's why Stein was considered a spoiler. This is not to say that Stein didn't have the right to run or that voters didn't have the right to cast their ballot for her. It is worth noting, however, that elections can be very close and by voting for a third party candidate who has virtually no chance of winning in a presidential race, you may actually be helping elect a candidate who does not share your views. Clinton lost and, in this case, liberal voters who chose Stein actually helped elect Trump, the conservative candidate.

What if I don't like any of the choices in an election?

Vote in primaries! Primaries are run by the parties, giving their voters the chance to pick the best nominee for the party. Except in states where there is ranked choice voting*, the party will come away with only one winner, who will then compete in the general election. Say you care about who gets that open Senate seat in your state, and you're a Republican. Voting in the primary means you'll be given a list of Senate candidates who are all Republican and you'll vote for the candidate you'd like to see as the Republican nominee. This is where you have the most choices within your party, and if you do some research on the candidates, you're bound to find one that aligns with your politics. If you sit out the primary but you still want to vote Republican, you will usually only have one choice in the general election. So find out when the primaries are, make sure you are registered by the deadline and that your registration is up to date, and then vote.

Remember, in some states you register to vote by party and can only vote in a party's primary or participate in a party's caucus if you are registered in that party. You may be able to switch your registration in time to vote in a particular primary and switch back later. In other states where you do not register by party, you can decide to vote in any primary, but only one. Check your state laws at vote.org. In states where voters register by party, you will be given the choices on your voter registration form.

Some state parties hold caucuses instead of primaries for the presidential election. You may be aware of Iowa caucuses that have historically kicked off the primary/caucus season and get a lot of attention because an early win can lead to positive momentum in other states. (In 2024, Democrats are beginning with a primary in South Carolina instead of Iowa, believing the demographics there more closely represent the country and the party.) Caucuses are in-person, and generally require a few hours of your time on a specified night. Participants hear speeches about each of the candidates and then stand in the space designated for their favorite candidate. If their choice doesn't get enough support, they have to choose another candidate. This goes on until there is one winner. The winners of each caucus in the state are combined to determine the final winner for the state party. Caucuses tend to have lower participation than primaries, but it is a good way to inform voters and help them solidify their choices.

*Ranked choice voting allows voters to rank every candidate on a ballot. There is one blanket primary with all of the candidates — from any political party or no party — and the top few advance to a general election. Thus, there may be more than one candidate from a party on the ballot in the general election. Counting systems differ, but in general, if a voter's first choice is eliminated, their vote would go to their second choice candidate, and so on. Maine, Alaska, and San Francisco use this system, and it's gaining momentum elsewhere. It's intended to be a more fair system that results in election winners who better represent voters. It also may discourage negative campaigning — hallelujah!

I've heard my vote doesn't matter because of gerrymandering.

Gerrymandering is the practice of drawing congressional or state legislative district maps in such a way that one party is almost guaranteed to win. Most of these maps are drawn by state legislators, with new maps drawn every 10 years when the new census is published. State legislators in the majority party at that time usually draw the new district maps. They have the power to redraw maps to their benefit, so many do. Some of the maps are extreme, with lines drawn house by house to include the specific voters they need to secure a win. They may also pack voters into certain districts so that the minority party will win one or two districts and they will win the rest. It's a lousy system for drawing district maps, and politicians have gotten good at manipulating it. Many states have had to literally go back to the drawing board because judges have called foul on the maps.

However, a handful of states, including California and New York, now have lines drawn by an independent commission, in an effort to be more fair. If your state has ridiculous maps (look up your state's congressional district map and the legislative district map and if you see lots of squiggly lines, you've got a ridiculous map), that's all the more reason to vote. Groups like the American Civil Liberties Union (ACLU) often sue to prevent unfair maps. They often present data on how many more votes a candidate received in a district over what they needed to win to prove that the district lines are unfairly drawn, and your vote needs to be in that data.

When lines are drawn so that one party is almost sure to win, elected officials don't have much incentive to please all of their constituents. Their party is almost sure to win again in the next election. They are entrenched. At this point, very few congressional elections in the United States are considered up for grabs. Most elected officials really only worry about a primary challenger from their own party. It forces some politicians to follow the party line even on issues they find objectionable because they fear the party will support someone else in the next election — and for congresspeople, that's every two years, so it's always right around the corner. It's worth your time to work against unfair district lines if your state has them so your congressperson can go back to representing you and your district, not the political party.

Note that presidential races, U.S. Senate and gubernatorial races are statewide, so district maps don't apply to those races.

I've heard my vote doesn't matter because of the electoral college.

The electoral college is widely misunderstood. It's only used for presidential elections, not elections for U.S. Senate and House seats, nor for state elections, such as Governor and state legislators.

In presidential elections, it is a way to give a voter in a tiny state as much say in the election as a voter in a large state. Here's how it works: Every state gets at least three electoral votes, one for each of its two U.S. senators, and one for each of its members in the U.S. House of Representatives.

To figure out how many U.S. representatives a state has, we rely on a national census every 10 years. The census is a count of how many people live in a state. The 435 seats in the U.S. House of Representatives are reapportioned in the fairest way possible based on population totals in each state.

Every state gets at least one representative, so states with very small populations, such as Alaska and Wyoming, get one voting member in the House. California, with the largest population, has the highest number — 52 Congress people (it lost one after the 2020 census).

In this way, electoral college votes are based on population, but even very sparsely populated states are important for winning the presidency. Wyoming gets 3 electoral votes, two for its two U.S. Senators and one for its U.S. Representative.

California gets 54, two for its two U.S. Senators and 52 for its U.S. Representatives.

In almost all states, the party of the candidate who won the most votes gets all of the state's electors. If the Democratic presidential nominee wins in California, all of the state's electors will be Democrats, and if the Republican presidential nominee wins in Wyoming, all of their electors will be Republicans. (There are two states that don't follow that rule, Maine and Nebraska. In those states, electors can be split based on the popular vote winners of their congressional districts.) Electors cast their votes for the candidate who won the presidential election in their state. It gets tricky when some electors feel they are not bound to follow the voters and can decide for themselves who will get their electoral vote. These are called faithless electors. Nevertheless, that's very rare.

Many people advocate for doing away with the electoral college. If it didn't exist, however, presidential candidates would spend all their time in the most populated states, such as California, Texas, Florida, New York, Pennsylvania and Illinois, and the fear is that those states could pick the winner. In fact, campaigning in just ten of the largest states would get you in front of more than half of all eligible voters. Why bother with tiny states such as Alaska, Wyoming, Rhode Island, or Delaware? Thirteen states and Washington, D.C., each delivered less than 1 million votes in 2020. Why address their concerns? The answer is the electoral college. Small states are guaranteed at least three electoral votes, regardless of how small their population is, and that gives their voters a boost. That's why the electoral college was formed, and why it's hard to abolish.

Does the electoral college somehow mean it doesn't matter if you vote? The answer to that is no. Your vote matters, whether you live in tiny Rhode Island or the most populous state of California. You contribute to the electoral count, and that's how presidential elections are decided.

I've heard my vote doesn't matter because I live in a red state or I live in a blue state.

Calling states "red" (meaning Republican-leaning) and "blue" (Democratic-leaning) is a disservice. All states are purple. Every one of them. Both parties exist in all states.

Never sit out because you think the winner is a foregone conclusion. In a "red" state, Republicans may sit out because they think their state is reliably Republican, it's in the bag, and their vote isn't needed, and Democrats may sit out because they think it's impossible for their candidate to win. Both are wrong. Elections depend on who shows up to vote.

In Texas — considered red — Donald Trump won the state by 800,000 votes in the 2016 presidential election. Yet more than 8 million people didn't vote. Was his win a foregone conclusion? Not at all.

"Red" and "blue" labels are assigned based on past elections, not current or future ones. Over time, voters in a state can change from liberal to conservative, or conservative to liberal. It all depends who votes and what the issues are at the time. If Democrats aren't energized one year and many decide to sit out the election, that will sway the vote. If Republicans are motivated by a certain candidate or issue, that may sway the election too. Of course, "swing" voters — those who vote for their favored candidates regardless of party, are often the most powerful. Some percentage of the electorate will reliably vote Republican, some percent Democrat, and the deciding votes will likely come from voters who feel free to choose candidates from either party.

Don't let red and blue labels keep you from voting.

Who is eligible to vote?

It's determined by state law, but in general, you can register to vote if you are a U.S. citizen, you will be 18 years old on or before election day, and you are a resident of that state. Many states allow citizens as young as 16 to "pre-register" so they are ready to vote when they turn 18. Laws differ by state on whether felons can vote, with some states allowing a restoration of rights after a sentence is served. People who live in the U.S. but are not U.S. citizens are permitted to vote in school board and local elections in California, Maryland and Vermont. Check eligibility requirements in your state at Vote411.org.

Okay, I will vote. How do I know if I'm registered? How do I register? How do I find my polling place? How do I vote by mail?

Every state manages their own elections and has their own voter registration laws. If you live in North Dakota, you're off the hook. There is no voter registration in your state. In some states voter registration is automatic when you interact with a government agency, such as when you get a driver's license. It's also easy to register to vote by mail — unless you live in Wyoming — using this national Voter Registration Application, eac.gov/voters/national-mail-voter-registration-form.

Be aware that some states allow you to register in person on election day, while many states impose a deadline for voter registration as much as 30 days before an election. If you don't meet the deadline in those states, you can't vote in that election.

To check whether you are registered and make sure your address is correct and up to date, go to vote411.org/check-registration.

States have their own voting laws as well. Some states allow you to choose in-person or mail voting, and some states offer one or the other.

Go to vote.gov for links to registration and election laws in your state, and make note of deadlines.

I can't make it to my polling place on election day, or I'm disabled, or I need instructions in a language other than English. What should I do?

Take advantage of early voting, offered in almost all states. You may need to go to a central polling place rather than the polling place you were assigned, and early voting will only be for a certain number of days, so make sure to check the dates, times and locations. If you will be out of state or otherwise can't make it to the polls, you may qualify for an absentee ballot that allows you to fill out your ballot and mail it. Some states require a valid reason, some do not. Find the laws in your state at vote.org.

For those with a disability, election officials are required to make polling places and even ballot drop boxes accessible. In locations where a sizable population speaks a language other than English — 10,000 voting age citizens or five percent of the total voting age population — federal law requires all election material to be translated, including ballots. That's the law, but if you find that it is not available, you can file a complaint with your local election office, district attorney's office, or the U.S. Department of Justice, Civil Rights Division here: civilrights.justice.gov/voting-resources.

Where can I get a sample ballot? I'd like to see it before I vote.

Especially if you are voting in person, it's a good idea to look over the ballot and make decisions before you get into the voting booth. Go to Vote411.org before an election and click "Find What's On Your Ballot."

What if I was given a provisional ballot or I was called in because my signature didn't match?

Make sure you follow the instructions given so you can prove your identity or fix your signature. Many people simply forget to sign their vote-by-mail ballot! You will have a short window of time to make corrections. If you don't follow up, your ballot will not be counted.

I voted. You happy?

Yes, but that's just the bare minimum. It's every adult's right and opportunity to learn what's going on and let your representatives know how you feel. It's impossible for lawmakers to know how policies impact every one of their constituents, so be sure to convey your personal experiences. Elected officials and their staff make note of incoming calls and emails and keep a tally of how their constituents feel on issues. You may persuade their vote on a bill or even inspire them to propose a new law. And if you need help, ask your elected representative for it. Providing assistance is part of their job. Say you've been waiting for your tax refund check for almost a year and it still hasn't come. Or you are a military veteran and the VA has denied you education benefits. Or you applied for a passport and it hasn't come in the time promised by the Department of State. Call your congressperson's office for help and their staff will get involved and work to solve your problem.

Now that I'm paying attention, I don't have a lot of confidence in my elected officials.

Run! That's right, any citizen can run for elected office, though to be president, you have to be a natural-born citizen, reside in the U.S. for at least 14 years, and be at least 35 years old. Start locally, maybe school board or city council. See if you like campaigning, listening to issues and complaints, and working with other elected officials who may or may not see things the way you do. See if you like talking to the media, and the ups and downs of public life. If you like it, and after you have served for a while, consider running for higher office.

You are an important part of our democratic republic — if you don't like how it's going, get busy.

I have other things to do. I don't want to run for office.

Donate to campaigns or groups working on issues that are important to you. Even small donations matter. They are the best way to advance your causes without running for office. It's perfectly fine to support candidates in your city or state, but you are not limited to that. You can send donations to any candidate for office in the entire country. The easiest way to find candidates to your liking is to go to WinRed (winred.com) or ActBlue (secure.actblue.com) or the website of your chosen political party.

You can support candidates you favor through individual campaign sites, but if your main goal is to help your party to win the majority in the U.S. House or Senate, here's the easiest way to go. If you want your party to win the majority in the House, donate to the Democratic Congressional Campaign Committee (dccc.org) or the National Republican Congressional Committee (nrcc.org), and the committees will allocate the money to campaigns within the party that need it most. To help win the majority in the Senate, the major party committees do the same for Senate campaigns: donate to the Democratic Senatorial Campaign Committee (dscc.org) or the National Republican Senatorial Committee (nrsc.org). Note that political contributions are not tax deductible for you personally or for your business.

You can also donate to political nonprofit organizations working for your cause. Chances are good they can really use your support. FYI, donations to groups that lobby for changes in law are not tax deductible.

Become an informed voter.

What does your country, your state, and your city or town mean to you? It can all change tomorrow, for better or worse. It depends on who voters pick to lead. You will live under the tone and priorities set by elected officials. You will live under the laws set by those officials, whether you like them or not. It pays to listen to debates, attend town halls, and read about the candidates.

Then vote!